THE TREE THAT RAINS

THE FLOOD MYTH OF THE HUICHOL INDIANS OF MEXICO

retold by Emery Bernhard
illustrated by Durga Bernhard

HOLIDAY HOUSE · NEW YORK

For our soul-sister,
María

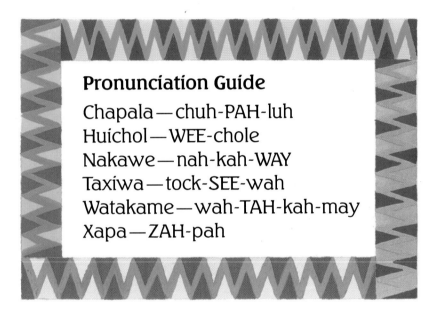

Pronunciation Guide

Chapala—chuh-PAH-luh
Huíchol—WEE-chole
Nakawe—nah-kah-WAY
Taxiwa—tock-SEE-wah
Watakame—wah-TAH-kah-may
Xapa—ZAH-pah

Special thanks to Peter T. Furst, Ph.D., Research Associate, The University Museum of Archaeology and Anthropology, University of Pennsylvania

Text copyright © 1994 by Emery Bernhard
Illustrations copyright © 1994 by Durga Bernhard
Printed in the United States of America
First Edition

Library of Congress Cataloging-in-Publication Data
Bernhard, Emery.
The tree that rains : the flood myth of the Huíchol Indians of
Mexico / retold by Emery Bernhard ; illustrated by Durga Bernhard.
—1st ed.
p.   cm.
Summary: With the help of Great-Grandmother Earth, Watakame, a
hard-working Indian, survives a great flood and begins a new life.
ISBN 0-8234-1108-7
1. Huíchol Indians—Religion and mythology—Juvenile literature.
2. Huíchol Indians—Legends.   3. Deluge—Folklore.   [1. Huíchol
Indians—Legends.   2. Indians of Mexico—Legends.   3. Deluge—
Folklore.]   I. Bernhard, Durga, ill.   II. Title.
F1221.H9B47   1994   93-8296   CIP   AC
398.2′089974—dc20

nce there was a man who loved to work. His name was Watakame.

Every day, from sunrise to sunset, Watakame worked in the fields. When he was not clearing, he was planting. When he was not planting, he was weeding. When he was not weeding, he was

harvesting. When he was not harvesting, he was praying for rain.
And when he was not praying for rain, he was clearing new fields.

Watakame did not have a wife or children, but he was not alone. On his rancho were five dogs, large and small, coming and going, growing fat on the scraps that he set out for them.

But one of Watakame's dogs never became fat, because she loved to work, too. This dog was black with a white neck. She followed Watakame everywhere.

While Watakame cleared the land, the black dog chased away the rabbits and squirrels. While Watakame plowed and planted, she charged across the fields scattering crows. At the end of the

workday, she waited patiently for Watakame to share his tortillas with her.

One morning, Watakame went to a field he had cleared of trees just the day before. He was surprised to find that all the trees had grown back overnight, including a huge fig tree that had taken hours to chop down.

Watakame shrugged. "I don't mind," he thought, "I love to work."
He sharpened his ax and cut down all the trees again.

Once more, the trees grew back during the night.

Four days in a row this happened, and four days in a row Watakame sharpened his ax and said, "So what if I have to clear the field a few extra times?"

But on the fifth day, Watakame complained, "I am tired of working in this field. I must find out why the trees are growing up as fast as I cut them down!"

Watakame and his dog hid behind a rock and waited.

At sunset, a little old woman holding a bamboo staff rose out of the earth.

She pointed her staff toward the south and the north, the west and the east, the sky above and the earth below. The great fig tree shot up from its snaky roots. And as Watakame watched, all the other trees he had cut down grew up, standing tall again.

Watakame grabbed his ax and charged at the old woman. "Old woman!" he shouted. "Who do you think you are? Day after day you undo my work! Stop casting your spell on my land!"

The stranger stood her ground. "Don't you know who I am? I am Nakawe, Great-Grandmother Earth, she who makes things grow. I have come to tell you that you have been wasting your time. The people have forgotten the gods, and a great flood is coming. In five days it will begin to rain, and it will not stop raining until your fields wash away and water covers the earth."

Watakame fell to his knees. "Great-Grandmother, what should I do?"

Nakawe smiled and patted Watakame's dog. "Do as I say, and I will help you. Tomorrow, cut down your fig tree. Hollow out the trunk and make a boat. Then gather five grains of corn of each color, five beans of each color, five squash seeds from your gourds, five fig seeds from your tree, five coals from your fire, and five squash stems to feed the coals. And bring this dog, too."

Five days later, a bitter wind blew and storm clouds filled the sky. As a heavy rain began to fall, Great-Grandmother Nakawe reappeared. "Are you ready to leave?" she asked.

"Yes, I have done all that you asked," replied Watakame.

"Load the boat and get in," ordered Nakawe. "Hurry, the water is already rising!"

Nakawe seated herself on the roof of the boat. The tiny ark began to float on the rising waters. Great serpents swam through the flood eating everything they could find, but Nakawe and her magic staff protected the boat and all that was in it.

The boat rode the waters, drifting for one year toward the south, for another year toward the north, in the third year toward the west, and in the fourth year toward the east. For one more year the waters rose.

Then the rain stopped. The oceans went down and the rivers went back between their banks.

The boat settled on a hill above Lake Chapala, where it turned to stone. Nakawe opened the boat. "You have done well," she told Watakame. "Now you can work again, and I can return to the earth to make things grow."

Watakame watched as Nakawe sank into the earth and disappeared. Then Watakame stepped onto dry ground.

Watakame walked to the south, north, west, and east, planting corn and beans and squash and fig seeds. He found shelter in a cave and made a fire with his precious coals. He prayed for rain and went to sleep. By morning the world was green with growing things. A great fig tree stood tall, gushing water from its shining leaves. The water rose into the sky and showered gently down onto Watakame's fields.

The black dog seemed to like her new home in the cave. When Watakame went off to work, the dog did not follow him.

One evening, Watakame came home to find fresh, hot tortillas. He ate most of them, but saved a few for the dog, who watched Watakame and wagged her tail while he was eating. Four days in a row, Watakame worked in the fields and came home to find food ready for him. "I wonder who is making these tortillas?" he asked himself.

On the fifth day, Watakame left the fields early and hid near the cave. He saw the dog come outside and look around. Then the dog took off her skin. Underneath was a small woman! The woman hung up the dog skin on a branch, knelt down over the grinding stone, and began to grind corn.

Watakame did not want the woman to put on the skin and become a dog again. Before the woman could stop him, he seized the skin and threw it in the fire. The woman cried out, "You have burned my skin and you have burned me!"

Watakame took some of the corn and mixed it with water. He washed the woman with the corn water, and she felt soothed and stopped crying. "I shall name you Taxiwa, which means 'washed with corn water,'" declared Watakame.

Watakame and Taxiwa were very happy together. They had many children. Soon there were people all over the earth, working and playing, praying and growing things...and telling stories about the flood just like this one.

And sometimes, when the people pray for rain for their corn and beans and squash, water gushes from the shining leaves of the great fig tree by Lake Chapala. The water rises into the sky and showers gently down on the fields, and the people remember how Great-Grandmother Nakawe and Watakame gave them The Tree That Rains.

 # Author's Note

Every year, in the cloud-capped Sierra Madre of western Mexico, Huichol shamans recite the flood myth at the harvest Festival of the New Corn and Squash. The people listen, eating the tender corn and squash that they believe have been granted by the divine mothers of the earth and by the rain goddesses.

Every year, Huichol Indians journey to Lake Chapala. With glowing candles they come to Xapa, The Tree That Rains. Huichol goddesses are thought to dwell in various lakes, caves, springs, and ocean bays—and it is necessary to visit them all, bearing offerings and bringing back containers of sacred waters.

Flood myths are found the world over, as are tales of humans whose spouses first appeared in animal form. The Huichols live on a mythical landscape. Although they are under pressure to enter the world of tractors and telephones, the Huichols still converse with the supernatural, and they continue to thank Great-Grandmother Earth—she who makes things grow—for the life she grants.

—E.B.

The pictures in this book were painted in gouache on Whatman cold press 140 lb. watercolor paper, with final touches added in colored pencil. The type is set in Kabel Ultra and Seagull Light extended.

2004